Try it out

Models and pictures have lots of uses. They help us to find out about things and to try out ideas. Models help us try things we can't do in real life – or just to have fun.

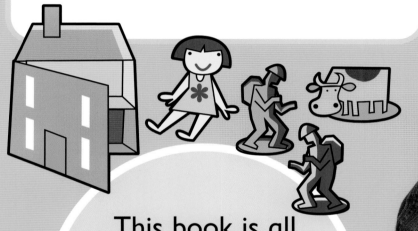

This book is all about different types of models and pictures on the computer and in the real world.

Making models

On the computer, you can play with models, and make pictures, too. You can try out things you can't do in real life – such as driving a car!

Getting dressed

A computer game to dress a baby is a kind of model.

To dress the baby you use the mouse to drag the clothes to the right parts of the body. It doesn't matter if you get it wrong. It is not like dressing a real baby!

A doll is another kind of model of a baby. It's more like a real baby than the computer game. It's hard to get the arms into the sleeves.

Dressing a real baby is much harder! It wriggles. You have to be careful not to hurt the baby.

Have an adventure!

In an adventure game on the computer, you move around a made-up world.

Make-believe world

In the game, you might have to collect tools, such as magic stones or swords.

You might have to fight monsters or hide from wicked witches.

What will I be?

You might have to be a different person or an animal. Maybe you can fly, or jump over huge rivers.

Making choices

When you play an adventure game, you choose what to do next.

If other people play, they'll make different choices. Then different things happen.

Models on the computer let us try out different choices.

Reality check

How like real life is a game? The characters don't get tired or need to eat. They don't argue about which way to go.

Looking real

Do you ever get cross if your own pictures don't 'look real'? Pictures don't always need to look real!

Getting it right

We all expect pictures to look real in some ways. But we all know they're not real.

Some types of picture, such as photos, seem more real than others.

It's not real

Even a photo isn't really like a person. It isn't warm to touch. You can't feel the person's clothes or hair.

We know what a cartoon is supposed to be – but it doesn't look very like the real thing.

What's the difference between a cartoon and a photo?

Practise!

Make a picture of a sheep. How can you make it look more real? Try it out!

Looking at pictures

Pictures don't only show us what things look like. They can show us what the artist thinks or feels about something.

Painting feelings

Some colours can make us feel happy or sad. In this painting most of the picture is blue and only the man's face looks real.

The artist has used blue to show us that he is feeling sad.

Does the colour blue make you feel sad, too?

Which colour makes you happy? Which colour makes you sad? You can use colour in your pictures to show feelings.

Practise!

Use crayons or pens of different colours that make you feel happy and sad.

Painting places

Some pictures aren't supposed to show us what something looks like. They show us how the artist feels about the place.

Can you see what this picture shows? It shows two trees next to a stream.

Paint a picture

You can make your own pictures on paper with crayons, paint or pens. Or you can make them on the computer with a painting **program**.

Think first!

Think about what you want to paint before you start. Ask some questions:

- What am I trying to do?

- Who will look at my picture?

- How will it be used?

- Should it be big or small?

- How much will I put in?

- Which colours will I use?

In your painting program, choose a paintbrush or a pencil and click on it. Now use the mouse to draw lines.

Look for brushes of different shapes and sizes.

Pick another brush. Experiment. It's not quite like a real painting – it won't smudge and the colours don't run if you go over a bit you've already painted.

Oops!

If you make a mistake, choose Undo to go back a step. That's not quite like a real painting, either!

Pick a colour

Bold and bright or pale and cool – colours bring your pictures to life.

Paint palette

Your painting program will have boxes of different colours you can pick. To choose a colour, just click on it.

Practise!

Draw lines in lots of different colours. What happens if you go over an area you have already painted?

Getting warmer...

Different colours have a different 'feel'.

 These are warm colours.

 These are cool colours.

 These are bright colours.

Spotty patterns

If there's a button for a spray can, you can 'spray' spots of paint over your picture.

Practise!

Can you paint candyfloss? A sparkler? A magic wand?

Try spraying one colour with the spray can. Then spray another colour over the top to mix them up.

All shapes

Painting programs make it easy to draw shapes and straight lines.

triangle tool

rectangle/square tool

oval/circle tool

rounded corner box tool

straight line tool

wiggly line tool

Looking for shapes

Find out which shapes you can draw. Can you find out how to draw these?

You can probably draw either filled-in shapes or outlines.

You can choose a colour for the filling and a colour for the outline. Find out how to do this on your painting program.

Full of colour

Find the **floodfill** tool. It might look like a paint pot. When you choose this, you can fill a closed area with the colour you've chosen.

Colouring in

Try drawing a pattern or picture with thick black lines on a white background and then fill in the areas with different colours. Can you make a picture like a stained glass window?

Or a painting like the one below?

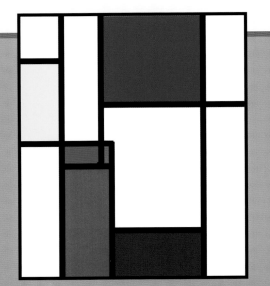

Practise!

Draw a picture from shapes made of black lines on a white screen. Then let a friend colour it in.

All change!

If you make a mistake, you can use Undo to go back to how your picture was before. But what if you change your mind much later?

You can paint over an area of your picture to change it.

You can also use the eraser to rub out a bit you do not want.

You can change the colour of an area with the floodfill tool. Make sure there are no gaps in the outline or the colour will 'leak' into the rest of your picture!

It's a good idea to save your picture first. Then you can go back to it if you don't like the changes you make.

Lots of tries!

Save your picture with a different name after you've changed it. Then you can keep both **versions**.

You can do this to try out different ways of making your picture. Or you can do it to make several pictures that are each a bit different.

cat 1

cat 2

cat 3

21

Stamp on it!

Using stamps can help to make your picture look more exciting. Stamps put finished bits on your picture for you.

Ready-made pictures

Pick the stamp you want to use and then click where you want it to be on your picture.

There might be different sets of stamps so that you can make different types of pictures.

If you want to make a scene like this, do all the background first. Then use the stamps on top.

Clip art

Another way to add bits is with pictures called **clip art**. They may already be on the computer or you can get them from a CD-ROM.

It's much quicker than drawing everything yourself, but you can still use your imagination.

Finishing off

You might think you've finished – but could you make your picture any better?

Look carefully

When you've finished, take a careful look at your picture.

- Is it what you wanted?

- You might want to change the colours, add something or go over a bit you don't like.

Add words

Maybe you could add a **label**. Look for a tool that lets you type words to add to the picture.

Blast off!

Show off!

Show your picture to someone else. They might see how to make it even better.

Save your picture before you change it. Then save it with a new name afterwards. You could do three or four and pick the one you like best.

Blast off!

When you're happy with your picture, ask if you can print it out if you want to.

Not all pictures need to be printed. You might make pictures for your school's **website**. People will look at the pictures on a computer.

Over to you

Now it's time to make a picture of your own.

Imagine you can design an outfit for yourself. It might be for a party, or for dressing up to be in a play, or for a sport you like.

Draw a picture of yourself. Choose a paintbrush and draw an outline, or you could use coloured shapes. It won't look exactly like you — but it's fun to do! Now save your picture.

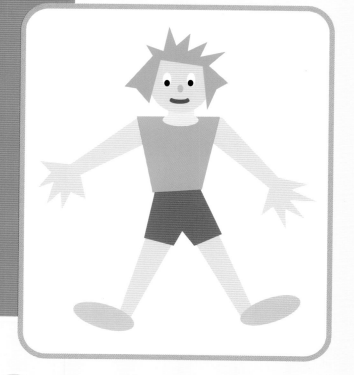

Start adding clothes. Use different shape tools and brushes to draw t-shirts, trousers, skirts, hats and shoes. Add patterns with a stamp. Use floodfill to try different colours.

When you're happy with your outfit, save it with a new name. Then go back to your body picture and make a new outfit. Save that with another name.

Make three outfits and then compare them. Which do you like best? Can you make that one any better?

If you print and cut out your body picture and your outfits you can make a paper doll of yourself. Leave tabs so that you can put the clothes on.

Be a designer

Designers often decorate the things they design to make them look nice.

Your turn

Have a go at drawing a design for something you use. It could be:

• a skateboard

• a bag

• a mug

• a book

or anything else! It's best to choose a simple shape.

The right shape

Start a new picture and draw the outline of the object you have chosen.

Save it with the name 'outline'.

Pictures or patterns?

Do you want a picture or a pattern? Which colours will you use? Is your design for you or for someone else? Make the design suit the person it's for.

Draw a picture or pattern in the outline and save your work with a new name.

All done!

Check your work, then print it out.

Is it a good design for the object you chose? Could you make it any better?

Glossary

character   Person in a story or adventure game.

clip art   Finished bits of art that you can add to your own work on the computer.

floodfill   Tool for filling an area of a picture on the computer with a colour.

label   Words added to a picture.

model   Copy of something in the real world.

program   Set of instructions for a computer to follow.

version   One form of something.

website   Set of web pages showing words and pictures that you can see on the World Wide Web.

Index

Grown-up zone

Making Pictures
and the National Curriculum

The work in this book will help children to cover the following parts of the National Curriculum ICT scheme of work: unit 1a, unit 2b.

It can be tied in with work on art and design.

Make sure a painting program is set up to make pictures of a suitable size. Provide stamps that are appropriate for the type of picture the children are going to make.

Children should have the chance to try out an adventure game on the computer which requires them to make choices or control characters. Get them to discuss the choices they made and the consequences of their choices.

Encourage children to work together and discuss options as they make their pictures. Review their finished work and ask them to talk about why they chose the versions they did choose, and why they rejected others. Ask them if they can think of any ways of improving their work.

Children should be encouraged to review, evaluate and improve their own work at all stages. If possible, show them work by older children and help them to see how this fulfils the same aims that they have in their own work.